Astronomy

Copyright © 1988, Raintree Publishers Inc.

Translated by Hess-Inglin Translation Services

Library of Congress Number: 87-28780

  2 3 4 5 6 7 8 9 0   91 90 89 88

Printed and bound in the United States of America.

Library of Congress Cataloging in Publication Data

Astronomy.

   (Science and its secrets)
   Includes index.
   Summary: Presents a variety of facts and myths about the sun, moon, stars, planets, galaxies, and other celestial bodies of the universe.
   1. Astronomy—Juvenile literature.   [1. Astronomy] I. Series.
QB46.A874   1988   520   87-28780
ISBN 0-8172-3080-7 (lib. bdg.)
ISBN 0-8172-3097-1 (softcover)

ASTRONOMY

Raintree Publishers — Milwaukee

Contents

Location of
Astronomical Observatories
Throughout the World

- Optical observatories
* Radio observatories

Mauna Kea Observatory

Pic du Midi Observatory

Zelentchouk Observatory

Parkes Observatory

How long have people been studying the sky?

People were interested in the sky long before the telescope's invention. Before that, they studied the stars' movements with quadrants. Quadrants were used to measure a star's position in the sky. Here, the ancient astronomer, Ptolemy, uses one (below right).

No doubt, prehistoric people wondered about the sky. You can imagine them standing in the entrance to their caves, gazing up at it. From their constant study of the sky, they probably learned many things. They probably knew the sun's route by the hour of day and time of year. Perhaps they noticed the moon's phases. At night they may have used the stars to guide them.

The first astronomical observations were recorded as far back as four thousand years ago. Astronomical observations are simply records or notes about what a person sees in the sky. The oldest observations are those of eclipses of the sun. Sometimes the moon moves in front of the sun, blocking its light. This is called an eclipse. The earliest records of eclipses are dated 2136 B.C.

In the Middle Ages, people did not understand the sky. They thought that it was a huge dome that covered the earth. The stars, they said, hung from this huge dome. This idea shows in artwork of the time. Here, a curious man breaks through the dome to the mysterious heavens beyond it.

Who invented the telescope?

Many people think that the great Italian scientist Galileo invented the telescope. Actually, he did not. But Galileo was the first to point the telescope toward the sky. As a result, he discovered many new things. These included the sun's spots, the moon's craters, Jupiter's satellites, Saturn's rings, and thousands of stars. Many of these things were invisible to the naked eye. The telescope helped people to see them.

No one knows for sure who invented the first telescope. Many historians say it was invented in 1608 by the Dutch lens maker Hans Lippershey. Lippershey did build and sell telescopes. He even asked for the rights, or a patent, to the telescope but was refused. Many people knew of the telescope. They had been working with lenses for many years. They had even experimented with magnifying glasses as early as the 1200s. In Lippershey's time, telescopes were already being built in several other countries.

Astronomers often see groups of dark spots on the sun. These spots, called sunspots, were probably first observed in China. There they were noticed when the sun's image was projected through the telescope.

Galileo demonstrates the telescope to the officials of Venice. Here, in St. Mark's Plaza, they view the marvels of the sky.

Finally, news of the invention reached Italy. Galileo built his first telescope in 1609. He cut his own lenses and put them into lead pipes. The first models magnified, or enlarged, an object only three times. But the most powerful of Galileo's telescopes magnified objects thirty times. Still, Venice's chief official was amazed when he first looked through the instrument. To introduce the telescope, Galileo had invited the city's officials to come and try it. Today, even the smallest telescope is much better than Galileo's. But though it was crude, Galileo's telescope changed the science of astronomy forever.

What is the difference between a refractor telescope and a reflector telescope?

The famous Mount Palomar Observatory is located in Los Angeles, California. It was built in 1949 and has a 164-foot (50 meter) dome. Inside is a telescope with a 16-foot (5 m) diameter. From this observatory many important discoveries were made. For example, the first quasars were seen from here.

Newton and the telescope

Sir Isaac Newton is best known for his theory of gravity. But he was also a genius in the study of optics. Optics is the study of light and its characteristics. Newton discovered that light is made up of the rainbow's colors. He also invented the first reflector telescope. This telescope was to have the greatest future. Newton's telescope was only 2 inches (5 centimeters) in diameter. Today, the greatest telescope in the world is 120 times larger.

A refractor telescope and a reflector telescope work the same way. Both have an objective turned toward the star to be viewed. An objective is a lens or mirror that gathers light. Both also have an ocular. This lens is nothing but a magnifying glass.

But the two are different. The refractor telescope's objective is a lens at the front of the instrument tube. The light rays from the star pass through this lens. They then come together at the telescope's back. There they form a single point called a focus. The image formed here will be enlarged by the ocular.

In a reflector telescope, the objective is a mirror. The mirror is placed at the bottom of the tube. It is covered with a thin coat of silver or aluminum. The mirror reflects the light rays toward the tube's front. The focus is there. But it is not possible to see anything from the front of the tube. (The person's head would be in the way). A second, smaller mirror is then placed in front of the focus. This mirror turns the light rays to the side. This design was Isaac Newton's. It is still used in some telescopes. The greater telescopes also have a second mirror. But here, the light is reflected toward the bottom of the tube. It is focused through a hole in the main mirror. Then the observer can stand behind the telescope. This telescope is used just like a refractor telescope.

In some very large telescopes, the mirrors measure between 13 feet (4 m) and 20 feet (6 m).

Refractor telescopes and reflector telescopes work the same way. Both take light and focus it in one point. There, the image is magnified, or enlarged, by another lens called an ocular. But there is a difference between the two. The refractor telescope shines the light directly through the magnifying lens. In the reflector telescope, the light is reflected through the magnifying lens by a mirror.

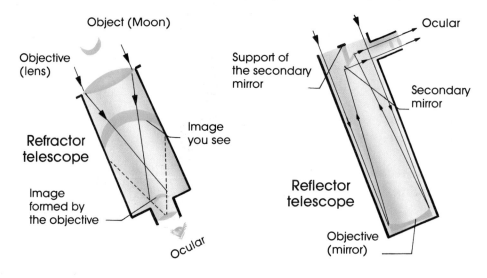

Which is the oldest observatory?

The first astronomers were scattered all over the world. At that time, there were no observatories. There was no common place for the scientists to gather and work.

One of the first observatories was built in A.D. 833 in the city of Baghdad. It was ordered built by the caliph, or ruler, Al Mamoun. There he began to gather information on the stars. Much later in 1260, enemy warriors destroyed Baghdad. These warriors, called Mongols, found another astronomical center south of Tabriz. This is now Iran.

Early astronomical temples were also built in Latin America. The best known is the temple of Chichen Itza in Mexico. It was built around 900 A.D. by the Mayas. The Incas, Toltecs, and Aztecs also studied astronomy. For example, they were able to predict the eclipses of the moon. (These eclipses happen when the earth comes between the sun and the moon. The moon is then cut off from the sun's rays). They also studied Venus' movements, and based their calendar on them.

The first Chinese observatories were built in the thirteenth century. The observatory of Kao Tcheng was built in 1276. It is one of the oldest. Every night, astronomers were placed on the observatory's towers. From there they watched the sky. They kept careful notes of all they saw. They recorded many comets and explosions of stars.

Today, these observatories are deserted or in ruin. They are not like the observatories used today. The ancient observatories had to count on human eyesight for their information. But these observatories were still valuable. The first maps of the sky came from them. Records of the stars and the movements of the planets also began here. The last great observatory of this type was built on Hveen Island, Denmark, in 1576.

The first great observatories were built in India. This one, at Jaipur, is still perfectly preserved. It has sundials set in giant stones. They are surprisingly exact.

Why are most observatories built on mountaintops?

Observatories are most often built on mountaintops. This gives the astronomer a sky as clear as possible. The Mauna Kea Observatory is the highest in the world at 13,780 feet (4,200 m).

The atmosphere is the great enemy of astronomers. Its movement is constant and often violent. This disturbs the course of light rays. It can also make observation of nearby stars difficult.

The air around the earth is very important. Without it, people could not survive. Despite this, the atmosphere is the astronomers' greatest enemy. They know of its importance. But they also know that the air disturbs the course of light rays. This does not cause a problem for most people. But it can make the astronomer's studies difficult.

The air is almost always moving. Its movement is caused by the wind, changes in the temperature, or other factors. This movement dims the light rays that come from the stars. This changes their images. Astronomers call this constant movement turbulence. In many ways, the atmosphere is like a filter. It blocks many of the rays given off by the stars. Only a few can get through the gas mass without being absorbed. Both light and radio waves can reach the earth. But other rays, such as infrared rays, are greatly absorbed. Infrared rays, often called heat rays, are like light rays. But they cannot be seen by the human eye.

Astronomers often build their observatories on mountaintops. This helps avoid the air disturbances. You may remember that the higher you climb, the less air there is. The less air there is, the less turbulence. High on the mountaintops, then, the telescopes and other instruments pick up many more rays. They record

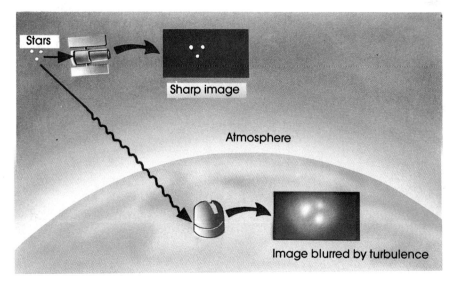

Stars

Sharp image

Atmosphere

Image blurred by turbulence

much clearer images for the astronomer.

A telescope set on Mauna Kea Volcano in Hawaii is one of the highest. It stands 13,780 feet (4,200 m) high. Another observatory is found in the Pyrenees Mountains. It stands on top of Pic du Midi at 9,439 feet (2,877 m) high. This observatory is known for its photos of the moon and the planets. They are among the best in the world.

these waves, the astronomer must use a radio telescope. A radio telescope acts like the aerial of your radio at home. It picks up the radio waves, which sound like faint hissings. The sounds are picked up by a recording device attached to the telescope. This machine traces the sounds on paper. The sounds are often in a zig-zag pattern. This shows how loud or soft each hiss is. The radio waves are also stored on a magnetic tape, as in a tape recorder. They can then be played back for study.

The study of radio waves has become an important branch of astronomy. But it began by chance in 1930. Then, an American engineer, Karl G. Jansky, found that his radio disturbances were coming from space. Since then, larger and more sensitive radio telescopes have been built. The greatest is at Effelsberg, Germany. It measures 328 feet (100 m) across and can be set in any direction. The United States built one in Puerto Rico that is 984 feet (300 m) across. But this one can only study stars that pass over it.

This recording from a radio telescope in Cambridge, England, is historical. It shows radio signals from the first pulsar discovered on November 28, 1967. Pulsars are small, rapidly spinning stars. They are called pulsars because of the short bursts of radio waves they send out.

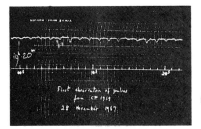

One radio observatory is found near Nançay, France. The main instrument there is this odd-looking wire fence. It is about 656 feet (200 m) long and receives radio signals from the sky.

What is a radio telescope?

Stars give off more than light. They also send energy, called radiation, in all directions. You know the sun shines because you can see the light it sends out. But it also sends out rays you cannot see. These include: infrared rays, ultraviolet rays, and radio waves. Ultraviolet rays are those that cause your skin to tan. Infrared rays give warmth. These cause your skin to turn red.

Most bodies in space send out, or emit, radio waves. To learn about

Which is the largest observatory in the world?

For a long time, the observatory of Mount Palomar in the United States was the largest. It is still the most famous. It was built at a 6,562-foot (2,000 m) elevation between San Diego and Los Angeles, California. Its mirror measures 16 feet (5 m) in diameter.

This huge glass eye was outdone in 1976. That year, Russia built a telescope whose mirror is 20 feet (6 m) in diameter. It is protected by a huge 196-foot (60 m) dome. It was built in the Caucasus Mountains near Zelentchouk, Russia.

There are now plans to build even larger telescopes. These will be from 25 to 33 feet (7.5 to 10 m) in diameter. But there are problems in building these large telescopes. The huge glass mirror can easily bend out of shape. This sometimes happens simply because of its weight. The mirror used in Russia weighed seventy tons. The future, then, is in using space telescopes. They are smaller, but they are outside the earth's atmosphere. Their photos are better than those taken from earth.

The telescope of Zelentchouk in the Caucasus Mountains is the largest in the world. Its mirror measures 20 feet (6 m) in diameter. The diameter of an object is the distance through its center.

Which are the most powerful telescopes?

The most powerful telescopes are those of Mount Palomar and Zelentchouk. They can "see" 600,000 times more light than the human eye. They can also photograph stars that the eye cannot see. Some of these are seventeen million times dimmer than the dimmest star that people can see. This could be compared to seeing a candle flame from 6,200 miles (10,000 km) away.

The range of these telescopes is hard to imagine. They can see galaxies further away than one billion light years. A light year is how far light travels in a year. It is hard to think about a light year. Light does not seem to take any time to get from one place to another. But it does. The further it must go, the longer it takes. In recent years, astronomers have found more stars. Some of them are farther away than ten billion light years.

Why are satellites sent into space?

You may remember that the atmosphere is the astronomer's greatest enemy. They built the observatories at great heights to avoid its constant movement and changes. After that, astronomers put telescopes on balloons. The balloons could climb 12 to 19 miles (20 to 30 km) above the mountaintops. There, the air is too thin for a person to breathe. At that height, the sky is dark even in the daytime. But the astronomers found that the balloons were not steady. Their telescopes could not gather accurate information.

Astronomers then dreamed of putting telescopes on satellites. Natural satellites are planets or other bodies that circle around another body. The astronomers' satellites would be earth-made space stations. They could be put into space beyond the atmosphere. There they would circle, or orbit, the earth like natural satellites. The first satellite, OSO 1, was launched in 1962. It went beyond the earth's atmosphere. There it studied the sun and the range of its rays. Such things could not be seen from earth.

Space is the best place for making observations. Since 1962, satellites with telescopes are used more often. More than fifty are now at work. New instruments are added to them all the time. Many of these are placed on the Russian station, Saliout. Some are used on the American space shuttles. Then the astronomers themselves make the observations.

In the future, the American space shuttle program will launch a new space telescope. It will be the greatest automatic telescope yet. From 310 miles (500 km) up, it will watch a huge part of the universe.

In the future, astronomers will have a fantastic new instrument for their use. A giant telescope will be placed 310 miles (500 km) above the earth. It will watch the sky twenty-four hours a day.

For centuries, the moon has fascinated people. At first, they considered it a goddess. It has always been a subject for poets and dreamers as well. In 1969, people walked on the moon for the first time. Since then it has given up many of its secrets. It now seems less mysterious. But this does not prevent people from dreaming!

How long has the moon orbited the earth?

Most astronomers agree that the moon was formed at the same time as the earth. Many rocks were brought back from the moon by the Apollo astronauts. Studies of the rocks show that the moon was formed 4,600 million years ago.

The moon has revolved around the earth for more than 4½ billion years. Some researchers agree that it is the same age as the earth. But they say it was formed in another part of the solar system. However, few astronomers accept this idea.

In any case, the moon has orbited the earth for several billion years.

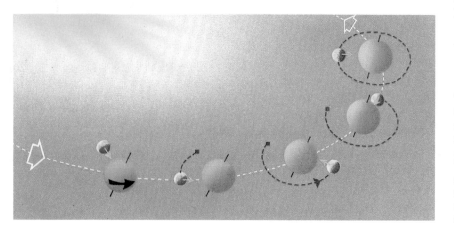

The moon is a natural satellite of the earth. Like most satellites, the moon circles its planet along a regular path. One such trip around the earth is called a revolution. While doing this, the moon also rotates. This means it turns itself completely around. The moon rotates once during each trip around the earth.

Why does the moon have a hidden side?

When you look at the moon, you always see the same side. One side of the moon is always hidden. This is because the moon turns once on its axis as it circles the earth. The force of gravity holds it in place.

To better understand this, try this experiment. Put a stool in the center of the room. This will represent earth. Ask a friend to sit down on the stool. Now, imagine that you are the moon. Slowly circle the stool. Always keep your face to your friend.

In your turn around the stool, your friend has only seen your face. Your back has never been turned toward the stool. But you have actually turned yourself around. A person sitting in a corner of the room would have seen you from all sides. You have just completed one turn, or rotation, of yourself. In the same time, you did one turn, or revolution, around the stool.

The moon makes one revolution around the earth in 27 $\frac{1}{3}$ days.

From 1969 to 1972, twelve astronauts walked on the moon in the Apollo program. Each time they came back, they were picked up from the ocean. From there, they were rushed into quarantine. This was done in case any germs or other organisms had come back from the moon.

For years science fiction writers wrote about life on the moon. Some imagined the moon's population to be like earth people. Other writers believed the moon to be full of monsters.

Is there life on the moon?

For years, astronomers doubted that there was life on the moon. They thought this long before astronauts ever walked on it. Through their work, they knew the moon had no air or water. Without these, life as they knew it was impossible.

But for many, many years, people have wondered about life on the moon. Without any scientific proof, they have often described its creatures. Centuries ago, the Greek philosopher, Xenophane, wrote his paper, "The Nature of Things." In it, he described beings similar to people living in the moon's valleys. The famous mathematician, Pythagoras, even imagined trees and animals on the moon. Even some early astronomers believed the moon had life. The famous German astronomer, Johannes Kepler, imagined giants living on the moon. These giants grew quickly by day, only to die by nightfall.

So before space missions began, astronomers knew that no higher life forms existed on the moon. Even so, American scientists were very careful during the first Apollo flights. The astronauts were quarantined for three weeks each time they came back. When people are quarantined, they are kept apart from everyone else. This was done in case they had come in contact with any moon organisms. Such organisms could have been dangerous on earth. They could have caused unknown diseases and spread quickly among the people. The earth would have been helpless against them. But tests done on materials from the moon proved astronomers right. The moon is a dead, lifeless world. No life ever existed there.

How many craters have been counted on the moon's surface?

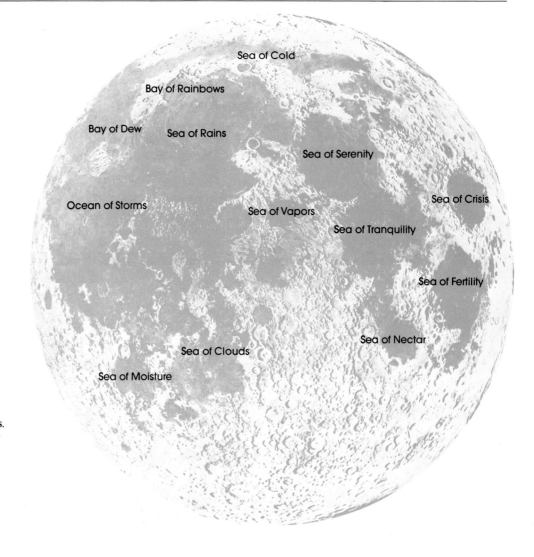

Sea of Cold

Bay of Rainbows

Bay of Dew   Sea of Rains

Sea of Serenity

Ocean of Storms

Sea of Crisis

Sea of Vapors

Sea of Tranquility

Sea of Fertility

Sea of Nectar

Sea of Clouds

Sea of Moisture

The moon's surface has many craters. As many as 200,000 of them are more than half a mile (1 km) wide. Astronomers have also counted twenty-four seas. These "seas" are actually great plains of lava covered with craters and rocks. They get their name from the early astronomers. Through their telescopes, the astronomers thought they were seeing seas like those on earth. Early geographers even put lakes, gulfs, marshes, etc. on their maps of the moon.

It is impossible to count all the craters on the moon's surface. There are so many of all shapes and sizes. Some are huge holes 186 miles (300 km) in diameter. Others are small holes dotting the rocks which cover the ground. Craters more than 6 miles (10 km) in diameter can easily be counted from photos. The others are much harder to count. The small craters are countless. An exact count for craters under a half mile (1 km) in diameter is impossible. But scientists can estimate their number. First, they count the number of craters in a small part of the surface. This number is figured for the moon's whole surface. The same method is used to count the stars in the sky.

By 1878, Julius Schmidt, a German astronomer, had begun counting craters. Using his telescope, he counted 33,000 craters on the only visible side. With a large telescope, you can see about 200,000 craters from the earth.

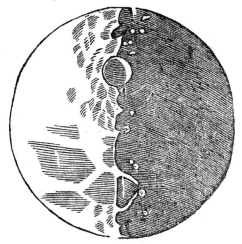

Galileo was the first to study the moon through a telescope. He made many drawings to record what he saw. Unfortunately, all of his drawings were destroyed except this one.

Are moon rocks different from earth rocks?

Moon rocks are not much different than those found on earth. But it is not really possible to find earth rocks exactly like them.

Rocks from the moon are generally all the same. There are two basic types. One is very crumbly, like an earth sandstone. The other is a crystal-like rock. It looks much like basalt. Basalt is one type of volcanic rock.

The moon's rocks were formed from a mixture of thirty-three minerals. The earth's rocks come from a mixture of over two thousand. There are no unknown minerals in the moon's rocks. They were formed from very few "ingredients."

The moon's rocks are all very old. On the average, they are between 3.1 and 4.6 billion years old. The earth's rocks are often much younger. This is because the earth's crust is always changing. But the moon is a dead world. Its crust has not changed since it was formed.

The astronauts brought back 846 pounds (384 kg) of moon rocks. Only a small part of these have been tested up to now. This rock comes from a lava plain known as the Ocean of Storms. It is 3.4 billion years old.

This photo was taken on July 21, 1969, during the Apollo 11 mission. It was taken by astronaut Neil Armstrong. Another astronaut, Edwin Aldrin, stands 98 feet (30 m) from the lunar module. In front is an instrument known as a seismograph. A seismograph can detect and measure ground movement.

What color is the sky from the moon?

The sky above the moon is totally black. This is true at night and during the day. You can see this in the photographs taken by the astronauts. The ground, the mountains, and the lunar module are lit by the sun. But the sky above the horizon is very dark. This is because the moon has no atmosphere. There is no air to

scatter the light. So, on the moon, only objects turned toward the sun are lit. The other side is in complete darkness. On earth, you can even see objects that are not directly lit. This is because of the atmosphere. Light passing through it is broken and scattered all over the earth.

Is it true that the sun is a star like the others?

It is hard to think of the sun as a star. Its light, its warmth, and its size make it seem so different from the rest. It does not match people's ideas of a star at all. Stars sparkle in the night sky. They can only be seen when it is very dark.

But the sun is a star. It only seems different because the earth is so close to it. The earth is 300,000 times closer to the sun-star than to any other star in the sky. If the sun were as far away as the North Star, it would be invisible to your eyes.

Astronomers are very interested in studying the sun. Because it is so near they can study it in detail. But people should realize that it is only a very average star. Compared to other stars, the sun could even be considered a dwarf star. Of course, there are some stars that are smaller. But there are a lot more stars that are much bigger. There are also stars that are colder. But many others are much warmer. In any case, life exists thanks to this star. You can understand, then, why people have worshipped it throughout time.

Average stars like the sun have some interesting qualities. Astronomers think that only average stars are likely to be surrounded by planets like the earth. Like the sun, only average stars can provide for life. It may be true that the sun is a star just like all the others. But it does have one important difference. It has a whole planet of people and other living things depending on it.

The sun gives the earth all of its beauty. Without it, the planet would always be in darkness. From other planets, the sun looks very different. From Mercury, for example, it looks like a huge disk. It looks 3½ times wider than the sun in the earth's sky.

How does the sun shine?

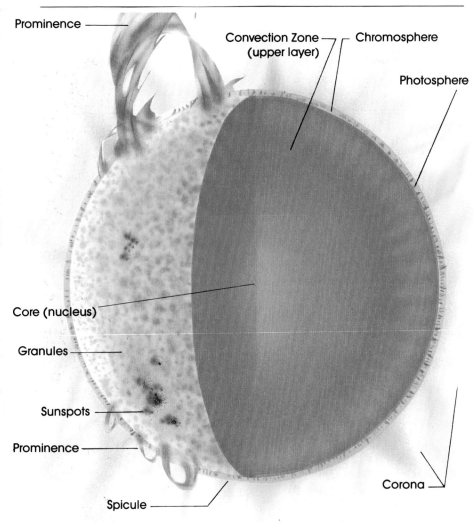

Prominence

Convection Zone (upper layer)

Chromosphere

Photosphere

Core (nucleus)

Granules

Sunspots

Prominence

Spicule

Corona

It is not possible to study the inside of the sun. But astronomers can guess what is happening there. These ideas, or theories, are partially based on what is happening at the sun's surface. The sun has a center, called a core. The earth's heat is made there. It takes the heat a long time to travel from there to the earth. Light and heat now reaching the earth were made in the sun's core 100 million years ago.

For many years, people tried to explain how the sun worked. Some thought it was a huge ball of burning matter. They compared it to a burning pile of coal. Others believed that the sun was slowly shrinking. They said its energy came from this. Still others said that falling meteors released the sun's energy. All of these ideas proved wrong. About a hundred years ago, scientists came to better understand the sun. They no longer thought the sun could be a burning mass. If it were, it could not have burned for more than a few thousand years. People have already existed about 2½ million years. The earth was formed around five billion years ago. Another answer was needed.

Finally, in 1938, an American scientist, Hans Bethe, and a German scientist, Carl F. von Weizsäcker, found a solution. They suggested that the sun, like other stars, is a mass of changing gas. It begins as a mass of gas called hydrogen. Scientists now know that the sun is about three-fourths hydrogen. This hydrogen is turned into another gas at the sun's center. This gas is called helium. During the change, the sun sends out huge amounts of energy. This energy is in the form of heat and light. This process is called a nuclear reaction.

What is the temperature of the sun?

The sun's temperature varies a lot. It depends on what part of the sun you are measuring. The sun's surface is called the photosphere. Its temperature is about 10,000° Fahrenheit (5,500° Celsius). You can imagine how hot that is by comparing it to other temperatures. For example, a furnace burns about

2,732° F (1,500° C). A kitchen oven reaches only 572° F (300° C). The sun's surface is made of small patches of gas, called *granules*. The granules make the surface look grainy.

Above the surface is a glowing halo. This is called the corona. It can only be seen during total eclipses of the sun. (It is not wise to look at the sun other times. The sun is too bright.) The corona is the sun's outer atmosphere. It has no edge. It just gets thinner and thinner as it moves away from the sun.

The sun's center, or core, has a temperature of about 27,000,000°F (15,000,000°C). The heat is made here. All the outer layers press down to the center. The great weight and heat make more heat.

Will the sun burn out someday?

When people look into a clear night sky, the stars are always there. They seem as if they will shine forever. Many people do not stop to think that stars do change. Like living things, they are born, they develop, and they die. The sun, which is also a star, will die someday.

The sun was formed 4.7 billion years ago. It formed when gravity forced gas and bits of dust to come together. In time, the dust and gas began to pack together tightly, or contract. As they did, they got very hot. The matter began to glow. After millions of years, the sun was hot enough for nuclear reactions to begin. In a nuclear reaction, the original gas turns into another gas. As this happened, the sun began to glow and give off great heat. It has not changed much since. Scientists

think it will glow this way for five billion years.

But one day, the sun will change. All the gas at its center will be used up. It will begin to burn its outer layers. Then the sun will become brighter and hotter. It will start to swell and change color. From yellow, it will turn bright red. At this stage, a star is called a red giant star. Soon all the planets will be within its burning range. Even the earth will be too hot for life to exist. It will burn to ashes at a temperature of close to 1,832°F (1,000°C). This phase of the sun will be short. Scientists think the sun will then shrink. When it is about the size of the earth, it will become a white dwarf. A white dwarf is a tiny, glowing star. It is all that is left behind by the red giant and is actually its core.

Scientists think that the sun will burn out in five billion years. It will then become a red giant star. As a red giant, it will grow until it has swallowed up all the planets. The earth will be burned by temperatures of 1,832°F (1,000°C). After that, the star will begin to shrivel. Toward the end, it will become a white dwarf. A white dwarf is a small, bright star that does not have much energy.

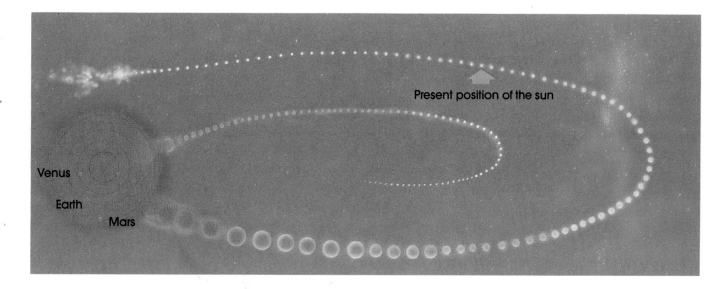

Venus

Earth

Mars

Present position of the sun

The moon sometimes gets between the earth and the sun. The moon is many times smaller than the sun. But it is also much closer. Because of this, it can sometimes hide the whole sun. This is known as a total eclipse. Total eclipses do not happen often.

What is an eclipse of the sun?

Seen from the earth, the sun and the moon seem to be the same size. You have probably seen this for yourself. The full moon seems to be the same size as the sun. But most people know it only looks this way. They know their eyes are tricking them. The sun is actually four hundred times bigger than the moon. It also just happens to be four hundred times more distant. This strange similarity makes the two bodies look the same size to your eye.

The planets and other bodies in space are always moving. Sometimes their movements create special situations. One of these is called an eclipse. Eclipses happen when one body blocks or hides another. Sometimes the moon comes between the earth and the sun. Then it blocks all or part of the sunlight. When the moon blocks the entire sun, it is called a total eclipse. During some eclipses, the sky is very clear. Then you can see the moon creeping over the sun as the two move into line. Soon the earth gets very dark. It is like night in broad daylight. Even the side of the moon facing the earth is black. (Remember, the moon itself does not shine. It only reflects the sun's light).

Each total eclipse can only be

seen from certain parts of the earth. The moon's shadow falls over these areas. It covers an area about 161 miles (260 km) wide and thousands of miles long. Total eclipses are one of the most interesting of natural events. But they last a very short time. The longest of this century was seen on June 30, 1973, over Africa. It did not last longer than seven minutes.

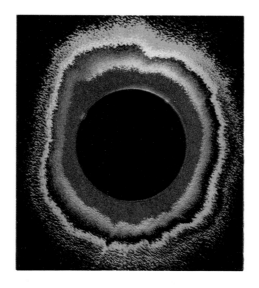

During a total eclipse, you can see the sun's corona. This silver halo cannot normally be seen. It is lost in the bright blue sky. But during an eclipse, the sky becomes dark. In this photo, the corona is seen as bands of different colors. A computer added this color to a real photo. This shows the temperature changes in the corona.

Why do dark spots appear on the sun's surface?

Sometimes one or several dark spots can be seen on the sun's surface. These sunspots often show on photographs of the sun. Astronomers in ancient China were probably the first people to notice the sunspots. But Galileo officially discovered them in 1610 with his telescope. With his telescope, he showed the sunspots to Pope Paul V and other church officials. The sunspots caused trouble between Galileo and the church. The officials could not believe that the "day star" could be spotted. They could not believe it was not perfect.

But the sun is almost always covered with dark spots. Most of the time, they are just too small to be seen. In fact, you can only see those which measure more than 25,000 miles (40,000 km) in size.

These spots mark colder areas on the sun's surface. Because of this slight temperature difference, the sun's brightness in that spot also drops. From the earth, this change appears as a dark spot. But why is it colder in some places on the sun's surface? Astronomers say it is because of a loss of energy. This happens when the sun's surface is pierced. The sun has a very powerful magnetic field, or force. The lines of this field, which cannot be seen, form rings around the sun. Sometimes the rings cut, or pierce, the sun's surface. Where this happens, sunspots appear.

Astronomers have been studying sunspots for many years. They have found that the number of sunspots varies. Sometimes there are many spots on the sun. At other times, there is not even one. Astronomers call this the sunspot cycle. A cycle generally lasts eleven years. During that time, the number of sunspots rises and falls. The high point of a cycle shows many spots. It is called a sunspot maximum. The low point shows no spots and is called a sunspot minimum. During the big maximum of 1947, the sun showed 107 spots.

It is very dangerous to look right at the sun. Even sunglasses do not protect your eyes enough. It is even worse if you look at the sun through a telescope. To study the sun, project its image onto paper.

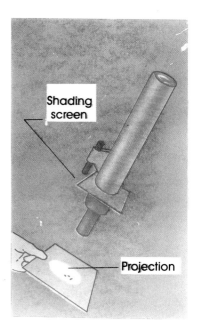

Shading screen

Projection

Are solar eruptions similar to volcanic eruptions?

Most people have seen photographs or films of earth's volcanoes erupting. During an eruption, the volcanoes spit vapor, ashes and lava. There are also solar eruptions. But these are not like earth's volcanic eruptions at all.

Solar eruptions, called flares, often happen near the sunspots. Small flares may last from ten to fifteen minutes. Larger ones can last several hours. Flares throw out much heat and light. The heat is about twice as high as that at the sun's surface. Flares also throw out charged particles. These particles are known as protons and electrons. They shoot out from the sun with great force. A day or two later, they may spray over the earth as they pass. As they near the earth, the particles gather in the upper atmosphere. There they hang in glowing curtains. These are called polar lights.

These flares start just above the sun's surface in the chromosphere. The energy caused by one of these eruptions is great. Luckily, most of this energy is lost in space. Only a very small part of it reaches the earth. The atmosphere protects the planet from most of this. But even small amounts are enough to cause problems on earth.

Another type of eruption on the sun is called a prominence. Prominences are great loops of gas that arch out from the sun. They shine brightly and last from a few hours to a few months. Some prominences shoot out in groups. Others are like long jets. The largest are big, arch-shaped prominences. A prominence may reach 20,000 miles (32,000 km) above the sun's surface.

Eruptions often occur at the sun's surface (see below). These eruptions throw, or eject, particles far into space. These glowing particles gather in the earth's atmosphere. They hang like bright curtains in the upper sky (bottom right).

What exactly is the solar system?

The earth belongs to the solar system shown here. It has one central star (the sun) and nine main planets including the earth. This solar system also has many smaller bodies. These include around fifty satellites, a belt of several thousand asteroids between Mars and Jupiter, and many, many comets.

The term *solar system* means "system of the sun." The solar system includes the sun-star and everything that circles around it. Nine major planets, including the earth, form a huge circle with the sun at the center. The system also includes some fifty satellites. Some are larger than the moon. Others are smaller. But most turn around the planets. Only the two planets closest to the sun, Mercury and Venus, do not have moons. Saturn, however, has the most satellites. Twenty-four have been discovered around it so far. It may have even more.

Small planets called asteroids are also found in the solar system. These form a huge ring between the orbits of Mars and Jupiter. The largest of these asteroids is called Ceres. It measures only 620 miles (1,000 km) in diameter. Eight of the other asteroids are between 186 and 620

miles (300 and 1,000 km) in diameter. But in all, astronomers have counted almost three thousand asteroids. Their true amount is much larger. There are countless asteroids of smaller sizes. Many of these are like big rocks. Some of them are not found in the main ring. The solar system also includes many comets. Comets have bright heads and long tails. Scientists think they are frozen lumps of gas and dust. They often come from far away. Some come from beyond the orbit of the furthest known planet.

But the solar system has more than planets, satellites, asteroids, and comets. It also has meteorites, dust, gas, and a wide range of particles. Even so, all of the elements in the solar system do not equal the sun. Together they represent only 0.14% of the sun's mass.

How long have all the planets been known?

The first telescopes did not have very good lenses. Astronomers could not see through them very clearly. To correct for the poor lenses, astronomers tried building longer telescopes. These longer telescopes were very hard to use. This telescope was built in 1645 by the astronomer Hevelius of Germany. It was 131 feet (40 m) long. It was so long that a wooden beam was used instead of a tube. It was only used to study the moon.

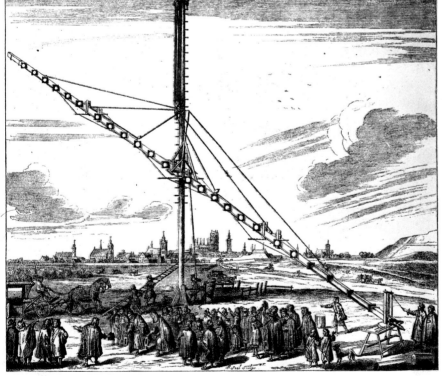

Besides the earth, people have known of five other planets for many, many years. These planets can be seen with the naked eye. That is how people knew they existed. The other five are: Venus, Mercury, Mars, Jupiter, and Saturn. The seventh planet, Uranus, was discovered in the eighteenth century. It is twice as far from the sun as Saturn at almost two billion miles (three billion km). It was discovered by the English astronomer, Sir William Herschel, in 1781. In the beginning, he thought it was a distant comet.

Astronomers studied Uranus' path for years. Often they found the planet was not where they expected it to be. It did not seem to move in a regular pattern. They then suspected that a large star was hidden beyond it. This would explain the pattern changes. The mysterious body was located in 1946 by the French astronomer, Urbain J.J. Leverrier. Leverrier used math to figure its position. He never even looked at the sky. Three weeks later, a German astronomer, Johann Galle, spotted the star. The "star" turned out to be a planet. But it was very close to where Leverrier had said it would be. The new planet was named Neptune.

The last planet, Pluto, was discovered by an American named Clyde Tombaugh. In 1930, Tombaugh was an assistant at the Lowell Observatory in Arizona. Like many astronomers, he believed there was another planet. Using other astronomers' figures, Tombaugh photographed the sky and studied the pictures. He finally found Pluto's image in three of them. Many astronomers think that there may be a tenth planet. If so, it is even further out than Pluto.

Is it possible to discover more planets?

Bodies in space affect one another. Often, they disturb each others' orbits. When astronomers see changes in a planet's orbit, they look for another body. Some planets, such as Neptune, have been found in this way. Neptune made changes in Uranus' orbit. But astronomers have found new disruptions while studying Uranus and Neptune. Some of them cannot be explained, especially those on Neptune. Pluto is too small to disturb either planet. For this reason, no one is sure that there are no planets beyond Pluto.

Some astronomers have tried to find a tenth planet. For now, they call it Planet X. It is possible that the sun could have more planets around it. Information from the Pioneer and Voyager space probes may help in this search. These probes will travel at the solar system's edge on their way to the stars. Like the planets, their movements can also be disturbed by other space bodies. The astronomers will study their movements carefully.

In any case, the sky was carefully explored in the search for Pluto. Through that, one comet and 775 new asteroids were found. Another planet could have been found during this search. Today's telescopes have become very powerful. More recently, new methods of space exploration have been used. Telescopes can now be put into space. This allows the study of very distant parts of the sky. New planets could be found in these areas. Many new stars were unexpectedly found. But so far, no new planets have been found. Still, the possibility should not be ruled out.

The British astronomer William Herschel built several telescopes in the 1700s. This one, for example, was 20 feet (6 m) long. With this instrument, he drew the first true map of stars.

Why are Venus and Mars called the earth's sister planets?

Venus and Mars are the two planets closest to the earth. They are the only ones in the solar system to have surface patterns and conditions like the earth's. The giant planets Jupiter, Saturn, Uranus, and Neptune are fluid planets. Their surfaces are not like the earth's.

Venus and Mars are also about the same size as the earth. Both planets also have mountains and volcanoes. On Venus, the volcanoes are even active. Venus is especially interesting to scientists. It is most like the earth in size, mass, and distance from the sun.

But Venus and Mars are also very different from the earth. Neither of them can provide for life as the earth does. For one thing, temperatures on the planets are poor. Venus' average temperature is 878°F (470°C). On Mars the average is -58°F (-50°C). The atmosphere on these planets is also very different. On Venus the atmosphere is very

Venus is surrounded by a thick layer of clouds. These clouds never break. For years, this has made Venus difficult to study from the earth. In recent years, space probes were sent to study Venus. Since then, scientists have learned a lot about the planet.

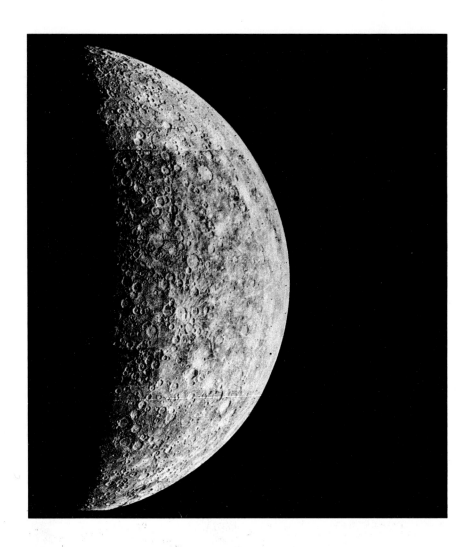

Mercury is the planet closest to the sun. In many ways, it is very much like the moon. It is covered with craters, and has no water or air.

heavy. Without protection, people would be crushed. On Mars the atmosphere is just the opposite. The pressure is very low. Finally, the air on these two planets is not good for human beings. Both are made mainly of carbon dioxide gas.

Which planet is the smallest? . . . the largest?

The evening star

Have you ever seen a very bright star in the evening sky? Many people call this star "the evening star." But the evening star is not a star at all. It is the planet Venus. It is often seen crossing the sky, between the earth and the setting sun. Then it looks like a large, very bright star. At other times, Venus can be seen in the early morning sky. It is then called the "morning star." At dawn or twilight, Venus is the only star to show. The others cannot be seen in the light sky.

Years ago, people thought that Mercury was the smallest planet in the solar system. It is also the closest to the sun. People know now that the smallest planet is also the farthest. This is Pluto. Scientists recently estimated its diameter at about 1,860 or 2,480 miles (3,000 or 4,000 km). It is not possible to be more exact because Pluto is so far away. It is only a point of light in the most powerful telescopes. In any case, this planet is smaller than Mercury. Mercury measures almost

3,100 miles (5,000 km) in diameter.

Jupiter is by far the largest of the planets. Its diameter at the equator is about 86,800 miles (140,000 km). Eleven earths put side by side would not equal Jupiter's width. Its volume is even more surprising. If Jupiter were a hollow planet, a thousand earths could fit inside. Jupiter alone has almost three times more matter than all the other planets put together. These facts are hard to imagine.

Which is the warmest planet?

Venus has the highest temperatures of any of the planets. This was shown by space probes that landed there. The probes always recorded temperatures between 842° and 896°F (450° to 480°C). The exact temperature depends on the area. On Venus, there is very little difference between day and night temperatures. Temperatures at the poles and equator are not much different either. This is because Venus is surrounded by a very heavy atmosphere. The heavy air keeps the temperatures even. The air on Venus is also mainly made of carbon dioxide. This traps the sun's warmth like a greenhouse. The surface temperature is always high.

Mercury is the closest planet to the sun. But it does not have the record for temperature. The temperatures on its lit side can reach 752°F (400°C). This is not much less than Venus' temperatures. But Mercury does not have an atmosphere. Its dark side can fall to -328°F (-200°C). This is the greatest temperature difference on any planet.

The atmosphere of Venus is made mainly of carbon dioxide gas. This traps the sun's warmth just like the glass of greenhouses. Because of this, Venus' surface is always hot.

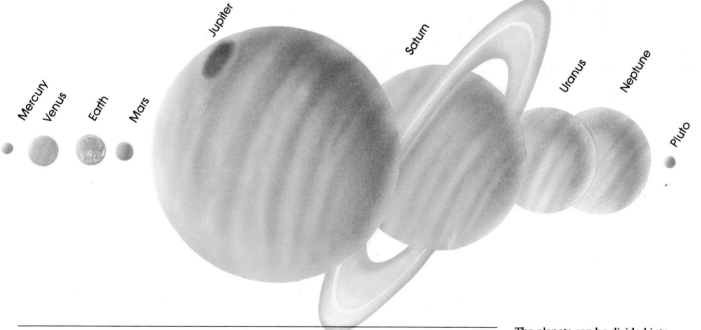

... And the coldest?

Pluto is the planet with the coldest temperatures. It is also farthest from the sun. Temperatures on Pluto are about -400°F (-240°C). It is a bare, cold planet. Neptune lies nearest to Pluto. It is not much warmer there. The orbits of these two planets overlap. At that point, they are about the same distance from the sun. From both planets, the sun is no more than a bright star. Only a very small amount of the sun's energy reaches these distant planets.

The planets can be divided into two groups. The first group is the giant planets. It includes Jupiter, Saturn, Uranus, and Neptune. These planets are made of gas and ice. The others, the terrestrial planets, are made mainly of rock and iron. This group includes Mercury, Venus, Mars, and Earth. Pluto is an exception.

Why is Mercury so hard to see?

Here, the space probe Mariner 10 goes through final checks in NASA's laboratory. It was later sent to Florida. There it was launched from Cape Canaveral on November 3, 1973. The probe flew over Venus and then over Mercury. The probe was able to make three close passes over this planet.

Mercury is the planet closest to the sun. From the earth, Mercury is always seen near the sun. Sometimes it is to one side, sometimes the other. But it is always very low in the sky. Trees and houses can block it from view. Mercury is best seen in the dim light just before sunrise or just after sunset. It is never seen against a black sky. This makes it hard to get a good view of the planet without a telescope.

Even with a telescope, Mercury is difficult to see. Light rays along the horizon must pass through a thicker layer of atmosphere. They are often absorbed in this thickness. But recent space study has solved this problem. Space probes see things from beyond earth's atmosphere. A space probe was launched in 1973 to study both Venus and Mercury. It took photographs on three passes close to Mercury. These photos brought new information about the planet. Astronomers now know that Mercury is much like the moon. Its surface is covered with craters. Like the moon, it is also waterless, airless, and without life.

Have space probes landed on Venus?

Yes, space probes have landed on Venus. Venus has more space probes than any other planet. The first probe was the Russian Venera 1. It was launched in Venus' direction in February, 1961. A year later, the Mariner 2 flew directly over Venus. It showed Venus' surface to be very hot.

In March, 1966, the Venera 3 landed on Venus. This was the first earth-built object to touch another planet's surface. Unfortunately, the Venera 3's radio stopped working. After it landed, it was not able to send any information to earth. The Russian scientists tried for a softer landing. They met this goal with Venera 7 in December, 1970. Still, the earlier probes had been useful. From them, scientists gained information on temperature and pressure on Venus. They also learned about the different layers of its atmosphere.

These first probes were not dam-

aged by the landing. The problem was in the great pressure and high temperatures on Venus. Several probes went to Venus after Venera 7. Even they could not operate longer than an hour after landing. Some of these probes were sent as recently as 1978 with Pioneer 13.

Of all countries, Russia has sent the most probes to Venus. So far, they have sent sixteen. Venera 9 and 10 were launched in October, 1975. These probes took the first photos of the planet's surface.

Over the years, many space probes have been sent to Venus. It has more probes on it than any other planet. In the future, scientists will send an earth-made satellite to Venus. This satellite will be the American probe Magellan. This probe will use radar to draw a map of Venus' surface.

Soviet probes Venera 13 and 14 took color photographs of Venus' surface. These were the first color pictures taken by probes. The probes probably landed near a volcano on Venus. Scientists have decided this from the rocks shown in the pictures.

Why is the earth called the Blue Planet?

People are used to seeing the earth in pictures like this. This is one of many photos taken from outer space. People forget that it was not always possible to take pictures like this. Only recently have scientists been able to study the planet in its environment.

From space, the earth looks like a huge, blue ball. You can see this in photographs taken by the Apollo astronauts. They took many such photos on trips between the earth and moon.

The earth looks blue for several reasons. For one thing, the oceans cover a large part of the planet's surface. In fact, they cover about three-fourths of it. The earth's atmosphere also adds to the color. The atmosphere is rich in nitrogen and oxygen gases. Both gases tend to trap and reflect only certain colors from the sunlight. In both cases, that color is blue. That is why the sky looks blue from the ground. It is the same in the other direction. Looking from space, the earth seems blue.

This is true of all planets with an atmosphere. In each, the atmosphere and surface type combine to give the planet a specific color. Venus is yellow. Mars is red-orange. Earth, of course, is blue.

Were signs of life found on Mars?

Astronomers began to study Mars after the telescope was invented. They soon discovered a world much like the earth. Clouds, deserts, and ice caps were seen. They also saw blue-green areas. These areas changed shape and color with the seasons, like earth's vegetation. They also found that Mars rotates on its axis every twenty-four hours. For these reasons, people began to imagine that Mars was another earth.

Before long, they began to wonder if it also had life.

Talk of Martians began at the end of the last century. Some astronomers saw box-like shapes on Mars' surface. The box-like shapes looked a lot like canals. It made people wonder if there might be intelligent life there. In 1965, the American space probe Mariner 4 flew over Mars. It was the first successful Mars space probe. It took twenty photos of the planet. Not one of these photos showed these canals.

One thing the photos did show was craters. Mars was covered with large craters. At first glance, it looked much like the moon. Like the moon, it showed no signs of life. Even so, scientists did not rule out the possibility of life on Mars. If there was life, however, they knew it would be a very simple form. Scientists wondered about the possibility of plant life or smaller organisms.

The Mariner 6 and 7 space probes later made new flights over the red planet. In 1971, Mariner 9 did a complete mapping of the surface. This probe was also the first to be placed in Mars' orbit. It took more than 7,300 photos of the planet in one year. The photos proved that no higher living things existed on Mars. Scientists now looked forward to the Viking space program. With this program, they hoped to land two automatic probes on Mars' surface. They hoped these would be able to test the Martian surface.

In July and September, 1976, Viking 1 and Viking 2 successfully landed on Mars. Both landed in the northern hemisphere of the planet. Each spacecraft had a pair of television cameras. With these, the Vikings sent back beautiful color views of the Martian landscapes. The probes also carried equipment for making many kinds of tests. The tests would be able to spot any life, no matter how simple. For these tests, the probes took samples of the planet's surface. This was done with Viking's mechanical arm. This arm's movements were controlled from the earth. The results of the tests showed the make-up of the Martian surface. But they did not show the slightest trace of life.

This photo of Mars was taken by the module Viking 1. Mars is seen here very clearly. Even the best earth telescopes would not give a better view. Notice the reddish color of this planet.

The Viking probes were the first to photograph Mars' landscape. In this photo, a probe sits on a model of its Martian site. There its different measuring instruments are tested.

In the film "Meteor," a huge asteroid hurtles toward earth, threatening to destroy it. In the end, the meteor is destroyed by Soviet and American nuclear missiles. The two countries unite to defend the planet. In real life, some asteroids can skim the earth. But none of them are big enough to destroy the planet.

What are asteroids?

Asteroids are chunks of rock that circle the sun. Asteroids are smaller than planets. The largest are a few hundred miles wide. The smallest may be only a few inches wide. Thousands of these chunks lie in a belt between Mars and Jupiter.

There are two ways to explain asteroids. Some people say that they are fragments of old planets. These planets exploded billions of years ago after the solar system was formed. Other people say that asteroids are rocky leftovers from other planets' formations.

Many astronomers follow the second explanation. They believe that the asteroids were always scattered, separate rock chunks. These astronomers also think that the rocks probably could have formed a planet. But they did not because Jupiter is in the next orbit. This giant planet's powerful magnetic force constantly pulls at the asteroids. It keeps them from sticking together. This idea is not impossible. Many planets in the solar system formed when whirling matter began to stick together.

But this explanation does not explain why some asteroids are made of different material. It does not explain why some asteroids wander out beyond the belt. Asteroids remain a great mystery even today.

Mars' two satellites and some of Jupiter's moons are probably captured asteroids. Those of Mars were photographed by the probes. They are very like asteroids. Also, some of Jupiter's satellites can switch the direction in which they rotate. This proves that they are not natural satellites. Natural satellites always turn in the same direction.

It seems . . . it seems like a big ball of fire . . .

It is a big ball of fire! . . . An ENORRRMOUS ball of fire!

Yes, it's a gigantic mass of matter . . .

And why is it growing before our very eyes? . . Because, it is growing, isn't it? . . .

Of course it's growing. It is coming toward us at a great speed . . .

It's coming toward us? . . . But won't it collide? . . .

Yes! . . . This meteor will collide with the earth!!

Heavens! . . . But then, it's . . .

YES . . . THE END OF THE WORLD! . . .

This adventure of Tintin, from *The Mysterious Star,* cannot happen. No asteroid in this solar system could cause the end of the world.

Could an asteroid skim the earth?

Ninety-six percent of all asteroids stay in the main belt. They spread out between the orbits of Mars and Jupiter. A small number of them, however, wander through the solar system. That is why some of them are found in Jupiter's orbit. These are called Trojan asteroids. They are named for the heroes of the Trojan War. Some asteroids wander even farther away. An asteroid named Hidalgo holds the record. Its course takes it millions of miles away from the sun.

Not all asteroids move away from the sun. Some have orbits that plunge them toward the sun. Some of them end up closer to the sun than Mercury is. (Remember, Mercury is the closest of all the planets.) One such asteroid is Icarus. Its path takes it within 19 million miles (30 million km) of the sun. It then moves out from the sun toward Jupiter. Eventually, these asteroids move back

into the main belt. But along the way, some of them pass close to the earth. One of these may one day crash into the earth. Such collisions have probably happened in the past. This would explain craters found on the earth. The most famous crater is Meteor Crater. It is found in Arizona. Scientists estimate it was formed 20,000 years ago.

Astronomers have studied asteroids for the last two centuries. In that time, they have seen some very close calls. Even near misses, however, cannot be seen without a telescope. The most famous of these was the asteroid Hermes. Hermes passed within 372,000 miles (600,000 km) of the earth. This rocky body is 1,969 feet (600 m) in diameter. The force of such a strike would be greater than the force of 10 million hydrogen bombs. This would destroy a good part of the earth's population.

The greatest of Mars' two satellites is Phobos. It is a rocky block about 17 miles (28 km) in diameter. It is not a true moon. It is probably an asteroid captured by the planet.

37

Of what are Saturn's rings made?

The center of American space operations is located in a suburb of Los Angeles, CA. In the control room, engineers and technicians watch the televised space images. These are sent by one of the Voyager probes from the vicinity of Saturn.

Through an earth telescope, Saturn appears surrounded by huge rings. The space probes have taken close-up photos of the planet. These photos show the rings' thin structures.

When astronomers first looked at Saturn, they were puzzled. Strange rings surrounded the planet's globe. From here, they looked like solid halos. But astronomers now know that the rings cannot be solid or of one piece. They know this because the inside edge turns faster than the outside edge. The astronomers now know that the rings are made of rocks, ice, and dust particles.

The inside section of Saturn's ring almost reaches the planet's clouds. It is thought to complete one rotation in about five hours. The outer edge of the ring stretches 43,400 miles (70,000 km) from the planet. It rotates in fifteen hours. The inner edge makes three turns in the time the outer edge turns once. These different speeds would have completely twisted a solid ring. In Saturn's case, it would have been twisted after one day.

Everything becomes clear when you learn that Saturn's ring is actually four separate coronas, or halos. You can see these coronas from earth. Each of these is actually made up of several hundred thinner rings. The Voyager space probes were able to take close-up photographs of the rings. These photos showed a total of one thousand thin rings. Each is formed by many small bodies. These include blocks of ice and ice-covered rocks and boulders. They form an unending belt of tiny satellites. These rings turn in tight circles around the planet. They are very thin. When seen "edge on," they almost disappear. But the widths of the bands vary. They range from 4 inches to 2 miles (10 cm to 3 km) thick. From a distance, these rings look solid. But astronomers now know that they are not.

Did space probes travel to Uranus and Neptune?

At present, the solar system has been explored as far as the planet Saturn. Probes flew over Saturn three separate times. These included the flights of Pioneer 11, Voyager 1, and Voyager 2. Pioneer 11 and Voyager 1 finished their missions. They are now traveling toward the stars following Pioneer 10.

The probe Voyager 2 was not finished. It continued its journey across the far solar system and headed toward Uranus. It flew over that planet on January 24, 1986. It is now heading in the direction of Neptune. This, of course, is even farther. The probe will reach that goal on August 24, 1989. After that it will plunge toward the galaxy's distant stars. It will head in the direction of Sirius, the brightest star in the sky.

The journey of Voyager 2 is the most fantastic one of any space probe. Hopefully, it will reach Neptune in good shape. If so, it will have seen four planets and forty-seven satellites. It will also have studied the solar wind and the particles scattered throughout space. It will have done all this and traveled billions of miles. The flight is already a success. The probe completed the first part of its mission. This called for the Voyager to study the two giant planets, Jupiter and Saturn. From its studies, it radioed back many photographs and measurements of these two. Scientists now wait for news of Uranus and Neptune.

Uranus is smaller than Jupiter or Saturn. But it is still one of the giant planets. Even so, from earth it is only a bright star.

The flight of the Voyager 2 is the most fantastic of any space probe. It was launched from the United States in 1977. Its route will take it over four planets in twelve years.

What is known about Pluto?

Many astronomers were surprised when Pluto was discovered. It was not what they had expected. Many were looking for a giant planet. Yet Pluto did not seem much bigger than the earth. Today people know that it is not even bigger than the moon. It is surprising that the planet was even found. In its corner of the solar system, it could easily have been missed. At the time, telescopes were much less powerful than now.

Astronomers studied Pluto's movement for years. They found it had an unusual orbit. It is far from being round. This orbit also carries it farther from the sun than any other planet. Pluto's orbit is also very tilted. All the other planets rotate more or less in the same plane. Finally, Pluto's orbit sometimes cuts into the orbit of Neptune. This has been true since 1979. It will continue for the next twenty years. All of these things made astronomers think that Pluto was not a true planet. Some suggest that it is an old satellite of Neptune. It may have escaped after being hit by a comet, for example.

These differences make Pluto a special planet. But it is a planet. Like all planets, it rotates around the sun. But its physical features and dimensions make it special. In many ways, it is a ball of ice and frozen gas. Its surface and make-up are more like those of a satellite. However, in 1978, it was discovered that Pluto has a moon. Pluto's moon is half as large as the planet. That is strange. Most satellites are much smaller than their mother planets. This moon, Charon, is also very close to Pluto. The two are so close that it is difficult to study the moon.

Here you see Pluto and its moon, Charon. Behind them is the distant sun. It is too far away to send much light or warmth.

What are comets?

In pictures, comets have heads like blurred stars and long, streaming tails. Actually, comets do not look like that all of the time. They look like that only while close to the sun.

The comet first appears as a fuzzy, bright object in the telescope. As it comes closer, the sun warms the comet. It thaws gases that have been frozen in solid crystals. The gases have been frozen since the comet moved away from the sun. These gases soon turn into vapor. They gather around the comet's head. By now the comet seems to be growing and getting brighter.

The gases soon begin to stream out behind the comet head. This forms the glowing tail. By now, the comet can be seen with the naked eye. As it shoots through space, the

Comets are beautiful when they are close to the sun. Actually, they are only big blocks of ice. Most of them are also very small. But as they near the sun, they are easy to see. Thawing gas forms the huge cloud and glowing tail.

tail grows longer and longer. A comet can even have more than one tail. These tails are sometimes very long. The record is held by the great comet of 1843. Its tail was 200 million miles (320 million km) long. That is twice the distance from the earth to the sun.

Before and after their turn around the sun, comets are small, bright points. They have blurred edges and are not much to see. Comets grow dim as they move away from the earth. Eventually they are beyond Jupiter's orbit. By then, you cannot see them without a telescope. This is because of the comet's make-up. They are much smaller than most people think. They only look big because of the gases around them. They are in fact balls of dirty snow. The American astronomer, Fred Whipple, called them "dirty icebergs." He knew that comets have a round core. The core is made of ice and rocky chunks. The largest is not more than a few miles wide.

From where do the comets come?

Comets may come from a huge ring of rock and ice found beyond the most distant planets. This idea was first suggested in 1860 by the Italian astronomer, Schiaparelli. A Dutch astronomer, Jan Oort, picked up this idea fifty years ago. He suggested that this mass of comets is found beyond Pluto. There, the sun's pull does not affect the mass much. But the giant planets, Jupiter and Saturn, do. The force, of these planets and of nearby stars disturbs the mass. Every now and then, frozen blocks break loose from the ring. These become comets.

Some comets are very beautiful. Many of these have long, sweeping tails. These are formed by pressure from the sun. As a result, the comet's tail always points away from the sun. This is true no matter which direction the comet is moving. This means that as the comet leaves the sun, its tail is ahead of it.

Comets circle the sun in strange paths. These paths are often very oval-shaped. As the comets move around the sun, they cross the earth's orbit twice. Their tails sometimes sweep the earth. Notice that the comet's tail is ahead of it as it leaves the sun.

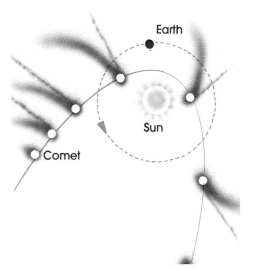

Comets come from very distant parts of the solar system. Some people believe a huge ring of comets can be found there. This ring would sit beyond the most distant planets. There the comets circle very slowly. They spend most of the time in very cold areas. The temperatures there are lower than -328°F (-200°C). From time to time, their orbits carry them toward the sun. They shoot around it, passing between and around the planets.

Is earth the only planet with life on it?

Vision and science-fiction. Here you see an artist's idea of a giant space city. It orbits the earth which is seen in the distance. Is this the world of the twenty-first century?

Many astronomers agree that other stars could also be surrounded by planets. It seems unlikely that planets would form only here and only around this star. For many reasons, astronomers think that other stars probably do have planets. But these other stars are very far from the earth. For now, scientists are not able to study them directly. Their equipment is not yet that powerful. Some stars do not move in straight

lines through the sky. Instead they follow winding paths. Their paths are disrupted by nearby stars. The gravity of other bodies in space pulls at passing stars. This is why their paths are winding instead of straight.

Satellites in space study the paths of such stars. Recently, one satellite detected solid matter near three of these stars. These solid masses could be planets. If these are planets, scientists would want to study them. Some of them might have conditions similar to the earth's. If so, they, too, could have life.

For a planet to have life, many conditions must be met. The right combination is very hard to find. But many people think that there must be many, many planets in the galaxy. Certainly some of these other planets have the right conditions. It is unlikely that the earth is the only one.

For the moment, no one knows which star might have such planets. But scientists do know that only one of the sun's planets has life. That is earth. Explorations with the space probes have shown this. In this solar system, the earth alone has life on it. That is now certain. But it is probably not alone in the universe.

Do UFOs really exist?

Thousands of people have claimed to have seen strange objects in the sky. People from all over the world have been spotting them for over forty years. These objects were first called "flying saucers." This name came from the shapes people described. Later, they were called Unidentified Flying Objects, or UFOs.

Most of these sightings can be explained. Very often, the person saw a natural event. These include certain clouds, ball-shaped lightning, or the planet Venus at its brightest. Other UFOs are earth objects. Things like probe balloons, satellites reentering earth's atmosphere, or planes and helicopters on military flights have been called UFOs. Some UFOs have even turned out to be jokes played by pranksters. Scientists have been able to explain all but about three percent of the claims. Often, in these cases, the people cannot give exact details. These cases make up a large part of the unexplained sightings.

So what do these hundreds, perhaps thousands, of mysterious cases mean? No one can answer. A true UFO sighting always surprises the witness. No good photographs have ever been taken. And no scientific information is recorded on the spot. So the study of UFOs is only the study of reports. Many of these reports come from everyday people. Often these people are not prepared to see what they have seen. So there is no real evidence for good scientific study. Still, scientists can gather some information from the reports. Their studies show the likeliest hours to spot a UFO. They also show which months and years had the most UFO reports.

In the end, many UFOs remain a puzzle. Even scientists admit that many UFO reports are truly strange events. The people who report them have honestly seen something odd. But these true sightings are only a small part of all reports.

No one knows exactly what to make of UFO sightings. Scientists have reports to study but no evidence. Photographs are rare. Most turn out to be jokes, or hoaxes. This photo was taken in the United States by a truck driver. It shows a hat-shaped object moving dust beneath it.

Scientists deal with all sorts of claims about UFOs. It is no wonder that it is hard to sort out the true sightings. People claim to have seen ships landing in fields. In some reports, strange beings came from the ships to speak to them. Then there are people who claim to have been captured by UFOs. Others have been contacted by beings from the spaceships. Sightings like these are not considered very possible. But this does not explain them all.

Some could be unknown natural events. Two hundred years ago, people did not know about meteorites. Others could be the result of people's minds playing tricks . . . a sort of waking dream. For now, scientists cannot say what UFOs are. They cannot prove that they are visits from outer space. But they cannot prove that they are not. At the moment, there are not enough facts to prove anything.

How are scientists looking for other beings?

The greatest radio telescope in the world is 984 feet (300 m) in diameter. It is set in the hills of Puerto Rico. In 1974, Americans sent a radio message toward the group of stars known as Hercules. This message is already more than ten light years from earth.

Even if UFOs exist, they may not be tied to visitors from space. But it is still possible that intelligent life exists somewhere else in the galaxy or the universe. Many people are interested in studying this possibility. Some have even tried to make

contact.

One of the first ideas was suggested in 1960. An astronomer came up with the idea of pointing a radio telescope toward a star. He thought the telescope might pick up an "intelligent" message. Such a mes-

sage might come from a planet circling this star. The idea was called "Ozma" project. It was the work of an American named Frank Drake.

The first test was done at an observatory in Green Bank, Virginia. The radio telescope was pointed at stars in the Whale and Eridan constellations. Constellations are groups, or patterns, of stars. These two are quite close to the earth. Their stars are similar to the sun. No message was heard.

To date, at least six hundred stars have been watched. Ten different radio telescopes have been used. Astronomers from the United States, Russia, Canada, Australia, and France have taken part. Together they have done over four thousand hours of recording. They have not heard even one message. But this is not surprising. Twenty or thirty years is a small amount of time. The earth has existed for five billion years. The astronomers may not have chosen the right stars to study. They might not have listened to the right channels. Their equipment may not yet be strong enough.

Distance is another problem. The distances between stars are counted in light years. A light year, you may remember, is one way that astronomers measure distance. One light year is the distance that light can travel in a year. Light travels 186,282 miles (299,792 km) per second. It is difficult to imagine such a speed. But you can see that a light year is a very long distance. It would take a message a long time to get from place to place. Imagine a message was sent from a star a thousand light years away. It would take a thousand years to get here. It would take earth another thousand years to answer.

So it may take awhile to get a

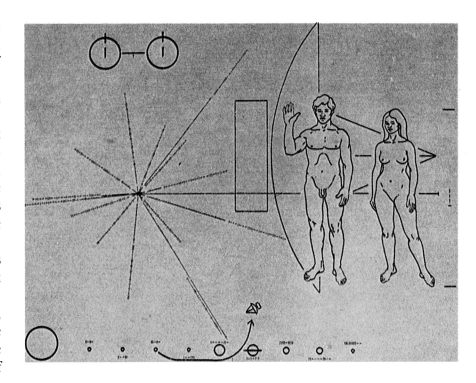

message if one is out there. In the meantime, some people have tried to send messages out from earth. To date, it has only been tried once. The message was sent from the giant radio telescope in Puerto Rico in 1974. A three-minute coded radio message was sent toward a group of stars in the Hercules constellation. These stars are found more than 25,000 light years away. With this message, the earth told the universe of its presence. It is possible that someone will hear this message.

People have made other attempts to send messages to other worlds. Messages were put aboard the space probes Pioneer 10 and 11, and Voyager 1 and 2. The messages were in the form of carved plates and disks. They are the first earth-made objects to leave the solar system. Their trip will last thousands of years and take them far into the galaxy. Sending messages into space is like throwing a bottled message into the ocean. These "space bottles" may one day be answered.

Here you see the first message written for extraterrestrial beings. The word extraterrestrial means something coming from beyond earth. The message was carved on this metal plate. The plate was then placed on the Pioneer 10 space probe. It went beyond the solar system in 1983.

The Voyager probes also carried messages into space. Some were more detailed than the simple carvings of Pioneer 10's messages. These disks contained images of the earth and its people.

The Milky Way is one of the most beautiful sights in the night sky. It can even be seen without a telescope. If the night is clear, it is very easy to see. Then it looks like a crowded band of stars. The sun and its planets lie at the edge of this band. From earth, then, astronomers are looking toward its center. Because of this, it is hard to tell one star from the next.

What is the Milky Way?

At the end of the summer, the night is sometimes very dark. The sky is perfectly clear. On nights like this, go as far from the city lights as you can. Then, if you look, you can see a long, white ribbon in the sky. It is not very bright. But you will know it by its size. It stretches from one end of the sky to the other. This is the Milky Way.

The Milky Way is a fuzzy band of stars in the sky. In some parts of it, there are only a few stars. In other parts, the stars crowd together. It is difficult to tell one from another. You can see all of this with binoculars.

The stars look like a huge mass when seen from the earth. People get this view because the earth sits on the galaxy's edge. This great mass of stars, including the sun, makes up the galaxy. Sometimes it is called the Milky Way system. There are more than 100 billion stars in it. They stretch across the sky in a huge disk. This disk is shaped like two plates turned against each other. From the earth, you are looking from the edge to the galaxy's center. That is why the mass of stars looks so thick.

What is a galaxy?

There are many stars in space. They are gathered in groups called galaxies. A galaxy also contains dust and gas. All of it is held together by gravity. There are many galaxies in the universe. Some are found alone in space. Others are found in groups. Each galaxy is separated from another by empty space. There are no stars and very little gas in these spaces. Astronomers do not know how many galaxies there are. Already, they have discovered many with their telescopes. In all there may be billions.

Astronomers are not sure how galaxies form. Some think it happens in much the same way as a star forms. Clouds of dust and gas come together. As the mass gets thicker, stars begin to grow inside it. Stars form in groups along the galaxy's edge. Single stars form in the center. The galaxy continues to form. Slowly, it begins to spin. Some galaxies spin very quickly. Others move more slowly.

The way a galaxy spins has a lot to do with its shape. Galaxies that spin slowly become elliptical, or egg-shaped. Fast-spinning galaxies become spiral-shaped. Scientists separate galaxies by their shapes. Spiral galaxies look like the Milky Way. They are like a disk with a bulge in the middle. These disks look like pinwheels. Their bright arms coil out from the center. The arms are full of bright stars and dark gas. Elliptical galaxies vary in shape from very round to very flattened globes. This type of galaxy has the oldest stars. It is brightest at the center. Most of its stars are found there.

The sun belongs to a group of stars known as the Milky Way. This galaxy is only one of billions of other galaxies. The Milky Way galaxy is a spiral galaxy. You can see its disk-center and curling arms. Many galaxies have this shape.

In a cross section, the center of earth's galaxy looks swollen (below). From face on, however, the galaxy has a different shape. Then it looks like gigantic fireworks with spiral-shaped arms. The sun is found at the edge of one of these (far below).

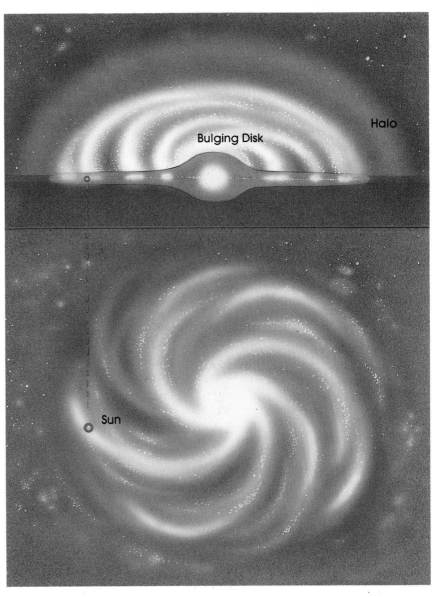

Bulging Disk

Halo

Sun

47

What are nebulae?

Photographs of the sky often show beautiful, colored clouds among the stars. This is especially true of photos taken near the Milky Way. These beautiful clouds are called nebulae. This word comes from the Latin word for cloud.

Nebulae are huge clouds of gas and dust. They have fantastic shapes. They are made of gas left over from the birth of a close star. However, they sometimes form after the explosion of a star. An exploding star is called a nova. When a star explodes, it grows very bright. It also shoots gas and dust into space. These then form into clouds, known as nebulae. Sometimes, the nebulae look like smoke rings. Other times, they look like huge balls. They often gather around the star that created them. Through a telescope, these nebulae look a lot like planets. Early astronomers named them planetary nebulae.

Sometimes, a star has a very great explosion. This is called a super-nova. Such an explosion makes a star billions of times brighter than the sun. It also destroys the star. Supernovas create nebulae with jagged edges. Nebulae from recent explosions are closely grouped in the sky. But some are tens of thousands of years old. These clouds are spread thinly. One very beautiful nebula (a single cloud) is found in the constellation Orion. It is a cloud of gas around four young stars.

The galaxy is made of more than stars. It also has a large amount of gases and particles. These gases and particles sometimes gather in clouds. In some places, close to a warm star for example, these clouds become very bright. They can then be seen from several thousand light years away. These are called nebulae. These clouds often surround stars in strange shapes. This is true of the Clover Nebula, (right) in the Archer constellation.

The early astronomers mapped out groups of stars in the sky. These are called constellations. The stars within a group are not always found near each other. Two stars that look close to each other may not be. They could really be very far apart.

What is the sky?

The sky is a huge dome above the horizon. It looks blue during the day. At night, it is black. All kinds of bodies can be seen moving across the sky. These include the sun, the moon, the brightest planets, stars, and sometimes comets. All of these things seem to be at the same distance from the earth. But it only looks that way.

Maps of the sky also look this way. Early astronomers traced what they saw in the sky. They mapped the stars in certain groups called constellations. But the stars of these groups are not really close to each other. They simply look that way from earth. Some stars in a constellation may be close to one another. Others may be very far away.

An example of this is the constellation, the Great Bear. Seven main stars form this group. In many places, it is also known as the Big Dipper. These stars only appear close together. Some of them are 140 light years apart.

People have used the stars to guide them for thousands of years. Grouping the stars in constellations made this even easier. The astronomers imagined lines linking the stars they could see. They imagined these lines forming people or animals from their myths. Each constellation was named for the animal or person it looked like. This helped the astronomers remember what part of the sky they were studying.

The name of the constellations

In 137 A.D., the Greek astronomer Ptolemy mapped the first constellations. There were forty-eight of them. The Greeks named them for people and animals in their myths. These names are still used today. These include: the Great and the Little Bear, the Swan, the Lion, etc. Early astronomers also split the sky into twelve areas or houses. The sun crosses through these areas throughout the year. These areas, and the constellations named after them, form the Zodiac. The sun, moon, and the planets circle through these areas. Maps of these constellations were first drawn in the seventeenth century. Since then, astronomers have added many more new ones. Many of the newer ones are named for birds or musical instruments. In 1928, the International Astronomical Union reorganized the maps. They declared eighty-eight official constellations.

How many stars are there in the sky?

No one can say for sure how many stars there are in the sky. Their number depends on several things. From where a person is counting them is one thing to consider. The sky looks different from different parts of the world. The time of year can also change the count. Remember, everything is moving in space. Some stars are hard to see at certain times of the year. What about the horizon? Forms at the horizon such as buildings, mountains, etc. can block a person's view. Finally, the quality of the sky is important. A darker, clearer sky offers a better view.

Ideally, it is possible to see 6,500 stars. But you cannot see both hemispheres at once. This means you actually see about three thousand stars. The sky may not be clear. The view might be poor. Or the moon's brightness may hide the stars. All of these things affect how many stars can be seen.

Telescopes reveal stars that cannot be seen by the eye alone. Counts done with a telescope are much greater. Even photographs "see" more stars than do human eyes. The greatest telescopes can photograph very dull stars. Some of these are thirty million times duller than those people can see.

It is impossible to count the stars one by one. The largest telescopes can reveal about five billion stars. But astronomers know that the galaxy has more than 100 billion stars. So for each star that can be seen, there are twenty to thirty more.

One of the most beautiful star groups is the Pleiades. It is about 450 light years away in the constellation of Taurus. Half a dozen of these stars are visible with the naked eye. A hundred can be seen with binoculars.

The names of the stars

The Arabs were the first to give names to the stars. Many of these names are still used today. Very few have been added to the first list. It is interesting to know how the stars were named. Take, for example, the seven stars of the constellation, the Great Bear. (Many people know this group as the Big Dipper.) Each of the stars is named for its position on the imaginary animal. These include: Dubhe (bear), Merak (hips), Phecda (thigh), Megrez (beginning of tail), Alioth (tail), Benetnash (crier), and Mizar. The Polar Star is named Alroukaba (knee).

A dome opens onto the starry sky at the Haute-Provence Observatory. For hours, it revolves from left to right, following the stars. Inside, the telescope always points in the same direction. In several hours, it takes one photo. It takes the film this long to record the pale light from distant galaxies.

Which is the closest star?

Proxima Centauri is the closest star to the sun. That also makes it the closest star to the earth. It is a small star. It belongs to the constellation of the Centaur. Many people have never seen this group. For one thing, the Centaur can only be seen from the southern hemisphere. Also, the stars are not bright enough to see without a telescope.

The Proxima Centauri is found about 4.3 billion light years from here. That is almost ten thousand times farther than Neptune and Pluto. A comparison might help you understand this distance. Imagine the earth as a pearl. The farthest planet would be 1,640 feet (500 m) from it. Proxima Centauri would be . . . at Paris.

Proxima Centauri is part of a system of three stars. These three revolve around each other. The main, brightest star is known as Alpha Centauri, or Toliman. It is one of the brightest stars in the sky. It has been known for a long time. The other two stars are less bright. One of them, Proxima, is a bit closer to the earth. This star was discovered in 1905.

People must remember that stars are always moving. They move in relationship to one another. In the past, there were stars closer than Proxima Centauri. Take, for example, the star called Gliese 894.3. This star is from the constellation Aquarius. About 700,000 years ago, it passed within one light year of the sun. This small star was then six times closer than Proxima Centauri. In 35,000 years, another star will replace Proxima Centauri. This star, Ross 248, will be only three light years away.

This photo was taken with an ordinary camera set on a tripod. A tripod is a three-legged stand that holds the camera steady. The photo shows hundreds of stars. These stars are invisible to the naked eye.

Is the Polar Star just above the North Pole?

Imagine a long line going through the earth at the poles. Now imagine this line continuing into space. Eventually, it would cut across the constellation known as the Little Bear. There, it would pass very close to the star called Alroukaba. This star is also known as the Polar Star, or Polaris.

The Polar Star can easily be seen with the naked eye. It is above the North Pole. It can only be seen from places north of the equator. So people in the Northern Hemisphere always know which direction is north. They must simply find the Polar Star overhead.

The star is almost directly in line with the North Pole. In fact, it is less than one degree off from it. But like all stars, the Polar Star is moving in the sky. At present, its course brings it very nearly in line with the pole. It will be even closer to it by the year 2010. After that, however, it will move away from the pole. Other stars will then take its place.

In about twelve thousand years, the star, Vega, will be the Polar Star. In the same way, other stars have also been the Polar Star. A star of the Dragon constellation was once the Polar Star. That was during the time of the pharaohs. This star may one day be the Polar Star again. As everything moves through space, the polar stars find their places again. The present Polar Star will one day point north again. That will be in the year 27,800.

Is it possible to see stars turn on or off?

Stars never suddenly go dark. When they die, they die slowly. They lose their brightness over several thousand years. A star does not disappear in a human lifetime.

However, stars can appear suddenly. Some show up suddenly where there was nothing the night before. But this is not the birth of a star in this case. Stars are also formed little by little over many, many years. Stars that appear suddenly are called novas or supernovas.

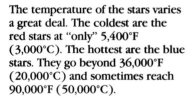

The temperature of the stars varies a great deal. The coldest are the red stars at "only" 5,400°F (3,000°C). The hottest are the blue stars. They go beyond 36,000°F (20,000°C) and sometimes reach 90,000°F (50,000°C).

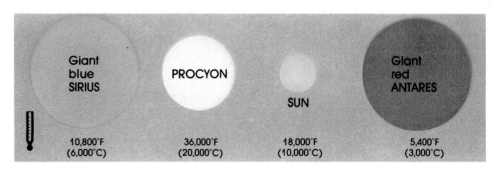

Giant blue SIRIUS — 10,800°F (6,000°C)

PROCYON — 36,000°F (20,000°C)

SUN — 18,000°F (10,000°C)

Giant red ANTARES — 5,400°F (3,000°C)

Which is the brightest star in the sky?

Sirius, the Dog Star, is much brighter than all of the others. Sirius is found in the constellation of the Great Dog. It is almost forty times brighter than the Polar Star. But it is only twenty times brighter than the sun.

Sirius is a blue-white star. It sparkles like metal, or like a diamond. It sparkles because it is always seen low on the horizon. There the atmosphere's layers are moving. Their movement makes the star look like it is sparkling. Sirius is also rather close to the earth. It is less than nine light years away. You can see it toward the south in the winter. It is best seen in the first half of the night.

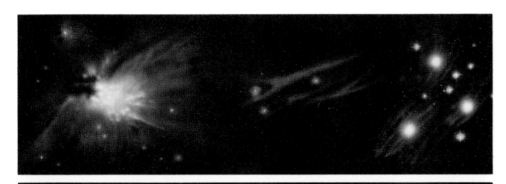

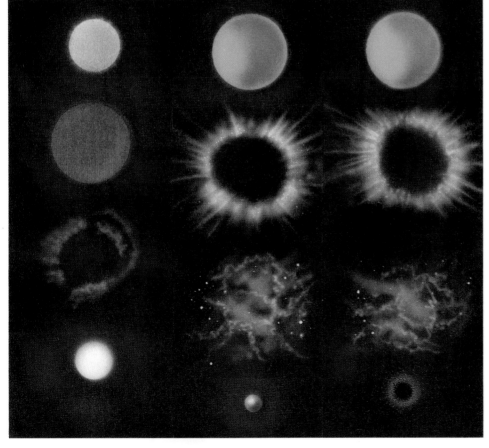

All stars do not grow old in the same way. The large ones change more quickly than the small ones do. They disappear after a few million years. A star like the sun is a small star. It will reach the age of ten billion years before it is old. Some stars become white dwarfs when they are old. This is a small, bright star that does not have much energy. Astronomers think the sun will one day become a white dwarf. Other stars explode into supernovas. They leave behind a core of matter. This matter can become a small spinning star called a pulsar. It can also become a black hole. A black hole is a star that gets smaller while its gravity grows stronger. It pulls things into itself. Nothing that falls into a black hole gets out.

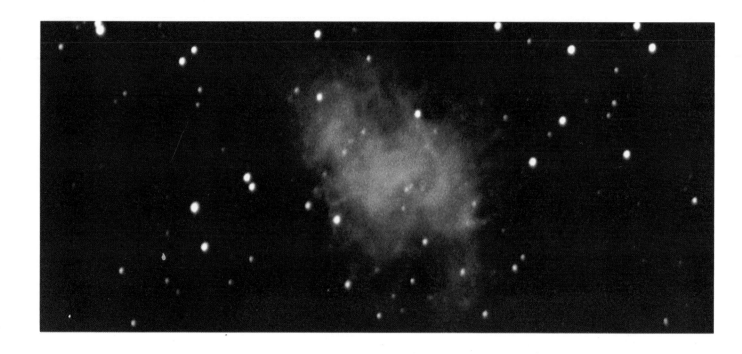

When a star explodes, it leaves a small core behind. This core is the size of a small star. It is called a pulsar. It contains about as much material as the sun. But the pulsar is squeezed into a tiny, wildly spinning ball. As the pulsar spins, strange clouds form around it. These clouds are the nebulae. They sometimes have beautiful shapes. The most famous nebula is the Crab Nebula of the constellation Taurus. This beautiful cloud was formed in July, 1054.

Can a star explode?

Only stars that have a lot of gas can explode. These are called supernovas. But then there are the novas. These stars pull gas from stars around them. This gas collects until the star suddenly explodes. Astronomers have now studied two hundred novas.

One fantastic nova was seen in the constellation of the Eagle in 1918. Before that, the star was too dim to be seen without a telescope. Then suddenly, it was as bright as Sirius, the brightest of all stars. Then its brightness faded. Seven years later, it was dull once again. In 1975, another nova appeared in the constellation of the Swan. This star grew as bright as the Polar Star. Before that, it did not even show on photographs. Even photos taken by the most powerful telescopes did not pick it up.

Supernovas are even brighter. They completely explode, destroying themselves. They leave behind small, spinning cores of material. The core of a supernova is called a pulsar. The explosion of such a star is very bright. It can sometimes be seen even in full daylight. Ten explosions of supernovas have been seen since the beginning of this era. They only happen about once every two hundred years. So they are rather rare. The last two supernovas appeared in 1572 and 1604. There should be one before the end of this century.

The most fantastic explosion of a supernova took place in 1006. It happened in the constellation of the Wolf. The exploding star glowed a thousand times brighter than Sirius. Another famous supernova was seen in 1054. This happened in the constellation Taurus. A gas cloud left over from the explosion can be seen there today. This cloud, called a nebula, has a ragged shape. (Nebulae from supernovas are often ragged.) This nebula is the very beautiful Crab Nebula.

What is a black hole?

When exploding, supernovas shoot their gases into space. They leave behind small, dense cores called pulsars. A pulsar contains about as much matter as the sun does. The pulsar's matter, however, is squeezed into a small ball. These balls are often no more than 6 miles (10 km) in diameter. To understand this, imagine a tiny piece of a pulsar no bigger than a sugar cube. A piece this size would weigh 300 million tons. This is about the weight of a small mountain. Now imagine a piece of the same size from the sun. This piece would weigh less than a third of an ounce (8 grams).

Now imagine that a pulsar is squeezed even more. The particles are already packed tightly. More pressure will crush them. Suppose you stacked eggs one on top of another. Egg shells are strong. They can stand the weight of other eggs being stacked on them. But if too many eggs were stacked up, the shells would break. This is what happens when a pulsar forms from a very large star. In this case, the pulsar begins to form as usual. The material is packed into a small ball. But because the star is large, there is too much material. But it continues to squeeze together. The star soon breaks under its own weight. Then the star becomes a black hole.

This type of star does not explode. Instead, it collapses inward. As it does, its gravitational pull grows greater. It begins to pull things into it. It is soon so strong that nothing can escape it. Even the light given off at the beginning is trapped. So it is also invisible. Astronomers describe this crushed star as a hole, of sorts. It is called a black hole because it gives off no light.

Astronomers are not yet sure that these black holes exist. They have not been able to prove that they do. Since they are invisible, they are very difficult to find. So scientists have tried to find them by studying unexplained forces in the stars.

Such a disturbance was found in the early 1970s. A star of the constellation Cygnus seemed to circle an invisible object. Astronomers believe that the object is a black hole. The star, called Cygnus X-1, is eight thousand light years from earth. At the moment, this is the only example scientists have. It may or may not be a black hole.

Recently, Walt Disney studios made a film called "The Black Hole." For the film, the studios tried to imagine a black hole. They tried to put what they imagined on film. Black holes are still one of the most mysterious things in space.

Will people someday travel to other galaxies?

It takes a very long time to travel to other stars. Future astronauts may have to be put into hibernation for the trip. It is the only way scientists can imagine keeping them alive. A trip to another star would last longer than a human lifetime.

People first appeared on the earth 2½ million years ago. Since their beginning, people have done a great many things. They have studied and explored the earth. They have probed and studied the solar system. They have even gone to the moon. It is not hard to imagine that people will someday explore the stars, too.

But this may not be for many, many years. The space probes take twelve years to reach the farthest planets of the solar system. The stars are even farther than these. It will take several tens of thousands of years to reach them. It has been that long since prehistoric people walked on the earth. Knowing this, it seems impossible that people will ever reach even the closest stars.

Scientists are still far from knowing how to travel this far. For one thing, they need spaceships that can travel at the speed of light. Scientists are not sure such a ship can be built. Today's ships are much slower. Even at light speed, however, the trip would take many years.

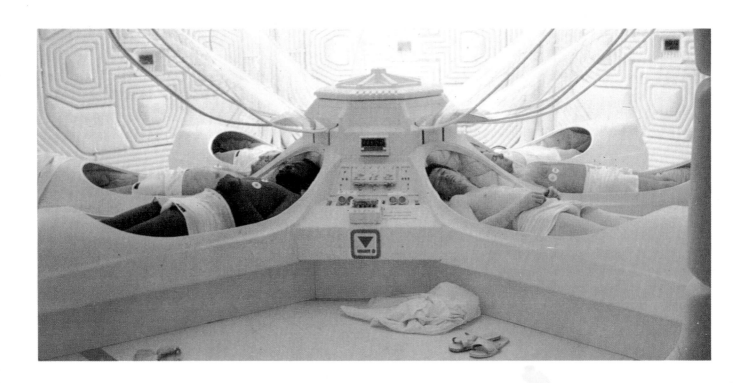

But these are not the only problems. Imagine that scientists were able to build a spaceship that was fast enough. Astronauts traveling at light speed would age slowly. But people on earth would grow old normally. The astronauts would reach the Polar Star only a few years older. In the same time, several centuries would have passed on earth. Would people on the earth still be interested in the spaceship? Would the country that launched it still exist? These trips toward the stars—or even other galaxies—are full of unknown adventure.

How far does the universe extend?

The great telescopes were invented around 1850. Before that, astronomers' views of the universe did not go beyond two million light years. This is the distance from the earth to the galaxy Andromeda. Andromeda is the most distant celestial body that can be seen with the naked eye. This is a great distance. But in only one century, astronomers have greatly enlarged this range. They can now see a thousand times farther.

The giant telescopes made this fantastic view possible. The one on top of Mount Wilson is 8 feet (2.5 m) in diameter. Another, on Mount Palomar, is 16 feet (5 m) in diameter. Both have improved astronomers' views of the universe. Photographic and electronic devices have also changed the view. Both kinds of equipment become more powerful every day. Finally, radio waves also help gather information from the sky. Today, galaxies farther and farther away are being photographed. Radio telescopes record their radiances. Some galaxies are found about one billion light years from earth.

In the early 1960s, astronomers discovered some very distant stars. These stars are not much larger than giant stars. But they give off as much energy as a whole galaxy. One star equals the energy of a hundred billion. These new stars are called quasars. Because they are so powerful, the quasars can be seen from far away. The closest of the quasars is found three billion light years from the earth. The light received from it is recorded on film. The light from this quasar is older than the earth is.

No one knows for sure what lies beyond the universe. Astronomers have noted that other galaxies and quasars are very far from the earth. The farther away they are, the faster they seem to be moving away. Scientists think this shows that the universe is expanding, like a balloon. Every part of the universe seems to be moving away from every other part.

The farthest stars that can be seen are twelve billion light years from earth. This is a short time after the birth of the universe. In a way, telescopes are machines for going back in time. A lot is expected of the great space telescope. The American shuttle will put it into orbit in the near future. It should be more powerful than all of the earth telescopes. With it, astronomers will view the first moments of the universe, fifteen billion years ago.

For the moment, the radio telescope is the only way to explore deep space. It is also one way to get in touch with other possible civilizations. Several radio telescopes are now constantly listening to the sky.

The Important Dates in Astronomy

285 B.C. The Greek astronomer Aristarchus puts forth the idea that the earth revolves around the sun.

127 B.C. The Greek astronomer Hipparchus compiles the first catalog of stars.

A.D. 137 The Greek astronomer Ptolemy publishes *The Almagest,* the first treatise on astronomy. It includes all of the discoveries made during the past centuries.

1543 The Polish monk Nicolaus Copernicus publishes a book demonstrating that the earth is not the center of the universe.

1609 The Italian scientist Galileo Galilei is the first to turn the telescope toward the sky.

1637 Galileo discovers the librations (real or apparent fluctuations) of the moon.

1656 Christian Huygens proposes that the protuberances observed around Saturn are a ring.

1659 Huygens draws the first map of Mars.

1664 Robert Hooke observes the great red spot of Jupiter.

1676 The Danish astronomer Olaus Roemer determines the speed of light.

1687 Isaac Newton publishes his master work containing his theory of gravity.

1705 Edmund Halley predicts the return of a comet seen in 1682 and several times in the past. This comet now carries his name.

1781 William Herschel discovers the planet Uranus.

1796 Jerome de Lalande presents the notion of "black hole."

1801 The Italian Abbot Giuseppi Piazzi discovers Ceres, the first asteroid.

1839 The first photograph of the moon is taken by Joseph Niepce and Louis Daguerre. These men also invented photography.

1846 Jean Galle discovers the planet Neptune.

1863 Richard Carrington is first to observe an eruption at the sun's surface.

1868 Jules Janssen discovers helium in the sun's spectrum. This gas was previously unknown on the earth.

1915 The distance to Alpha Centauri, the closest star, is calculated at more than four light years.

1918 Harlow Shapley determines the shape of the galaxy.

1930 Clyde Tombaugh discovers the planet Pluto.

1931 Karl Jansky discovers the radio emissions of the Milky Way. Six years later, Grote Reber builds the first true radio telescope.

1938 Hans Bethe explains the origin of the radiance of the sun and of the stars by thermonuclear fusion.

1957 U.S.S.R. launches *Sputnik I,* the first earth satellite.

1959 The first photographs of the moon's hidden side are taken by the Russian probe Luna 3.

1966 Automatic space probes are sucessfully placed on the moon.

1967 Jocelyn Bell discovers pulsars.

1969 Astronaut Neil Armstrong walks on the moon.

1972 The Russian probe Venera 7 lands on Venus.

1973 The American space probe Pioneer 10 completes first flight over Jupiter.

1974 The American space probe Mariner 10 completes first flight over Mercury.

1975 The Russian probe Venera 9 takes the first close-up photographs of Venus.

1977 J. Elliott and his team discover the rings of Uranus.

1978 J. Christy discovers a satellite around Pluto.

1979 The American space probe Pioneer 11 completes first flight over Saturn.

1984 Svetlana Sabitskaya becomes the first woman to "walk" in space.

1986 U.S. *Voyager* flies past Uranus, sending back pictures and data.

The Largest Observatories in the World

Name	Location	Country Using It	Diameter of Main Telescope	Year Telescope Established
Zelentchouk	Caucasus	Russia	236 inches (600 cm)	1976
Palomar	California	United States	200 inches (508 cm)	1949
Mount Hopkins	Arizona	United States	177 inches (450 cm)	1979
Roque de los Muchachos	Canary Islands	Spain/ Great Britain	177 inches (450 cm)	1984
Kitt Peak	Arizona	United States	158 inches (401 cm)	1973
Cerro Tololo	Chile	United States	158 inches (401 cm)	1975
Siding Spring	Australia	Great Britain/ Australia	154 inches (391 cm)	1974
Mauna Kea	Hawaii	France/ Canada	144 inches (366 cm)	1979
La Silla	Chile	Europe	142 inches (360 cm)	1976
Calar Alto	Spain	Spain/ West Germany	138 inches (350 cm)	1984
Lick	California	United States	120 inches (305 cm)	1959
McDonald	Texas	United States	107 inches (273 cm)	1968

Glossary

artificial satellite   an object or vehicle made on earth which is intended to orbit the earth, the moon, or other celestial body. Artificial satellites are used in astronomical study. They may be used to spot solar storms, measure stars' warmth, watch the weather, or for many other tasks.

asteroids   pieces of rock that circle the sun. There are thousands of asteroids between Jupiter and Mars. Asteroids range in size from less than a mile across to about 500 miles (805 km) across.

astronomy   the study of the universe. Astronomy is especially interested in the observation and interpretation of the positions, motion, and composition of the celestial bodies.

atmosphere   the gaseous mass surrounding the earth or other celestial body.

black hole   the matter that is finally left after a very large star has had a supernova explosion.

comet   a body in space that has a bright head and long glowing tail.

constellation   one of the eighty-eight star patterns that are on the map of the sky.

corona   the outermost part of the sun's atmosphere. The corona can only be seen during an eclipse. Then it appears as a glowing halo.

eclipse   when one body in space blocks, or partially blocks, another. An eclipse of the sun occurs when the moon moves between the sun and earth and blocks the sun from view. An eclipse of the moon occurs when the earth is between the sun and the moon and the earth's shadow blocks the moon from view.

flare   an eruption on the sun's surface. During a flare, much heat and light are thrown out. Protons and electrons are also thrown from the surface.

galaxy   one of the large groups of bodies in the universe. Most of the bodies in a galaxy are stars. There may be billions of stars in each galaxy in the universe.

light year   the distance that light travels in one year. Light travels at about 186,000 miles per second (299,274 km).

meteor   a piece of matter that is floating in the solar system. A meteor becomes visible when it enters the earth's atmosphere.

meteorite   a piece of matter from space that lands on earth.

Milky Way   a band of light that stretches from one end of the sky to the other. The Milky Way is actually made up of billions of faint stars.

nebula   an immense cloud of glowing gases and dust in space.

nova   a star that explodes and emits gases and dust. During the explosion, the star is thousands of times brighter than it normally is. After a period of months, or even years, the star goes back to its original brightness.

observatory   a building equipped to make astronomical studies. An astronomical observatory often houses a telescope under a large dome. For viewing purposes, the dome can open, and the telescope can swing around inside of it.

ocular   the eyepiece of an optical instrument. The ocular of a telescope is the part through which an image is seen and magnified.

prominence   a mass of glowing gas that has erupted from the sun's surface.

pulsar   the core of matter that is left behind after a supernova explosion.

quasar   a star-like body that has as much energy as billions of normal stars. Quasars are much farther away than stars.

radio telescope   an instrument used to collect and study the radio waves given off by objects in space. A radio telescope acts like a car antenna. It collects radio waves the way an optical telescope collects light.

red giant   a star that gives off a red glow because of a low surface temperature. Giant stars are larger and brighter than "ordinary" stars like the sun. They are also different in pressure and density.

reflector telescope   a telescope in which the image being viewed bounces off a mirror at the rear of the telescope and is focused at the front of the telescope.

refractor telescope   a telescope that has a lens at its front. That lens focuses the image being viewed at the rear of the telescope. Another lens at the rear magnifies the image, making it seem closer that it actually is.

satellite   a body in space that revolves around another, larger body.

solar system   the sun and all the bodies that revolve around it, including the planets and their satellites, or moons.

space probe   an object that is sent into space in order to send back information.

sunspot   an area, or spot, on the sun's surface that is darker than the surrounding area. Sunspots occur because those areas are colder than other parts of the surface. Because the temperature is lower, the area is less bright.

supernova   a star that explodes and becomes billions of times brighter than it normally is.

telescope   an instrument that is used for viewing distant objects.

white dwarf   a small star that does not have much energy.

INDEX